Piano ■ Vocal ■ Guitar

MAROON 5
RED PILL BLUES

ISBN 978-1-5400-2036-9

7777 W. BLUEMOUND RD. P.O. BOX 13819 MILWAUKEE, WI 53213

In Australia Contact:
Hal Leonard Australia Pty. Ltd.
4 Lentara Court
Cheltenham, Victoria, 3192 Australia
Email: ausadmin@halleonard.com.au

Visit Hal Leonard Online at
www.halleonard.com

BEST 4 U

Words and Music by ADAM LEVINE,
JULIAN BUNETTA, IAN FRANZINO,
ANDREW HAAS, JACOB KASHER HINDLIN,
ALEXANDER IZQUIERDO and JOHN RYAN

* *Recorded a half step higher.*

WHAT LOVERS DO

Words and Music by ADAM LEVINE,
SOLANA ROWE, JASON EVIGAN,
OLADAYO OLATUNJI, BRITTANY HAZZARD,
VICTOR RAADSTROM and BEN DIEHL

WAIT

Words and Music by ADAM LEVINE,
JACOB KASHER HINDLIN, AMMAR MALIK
and JOHN RYAN

To Coda

wait; could you come in, please, 'cause I wan-na be with you. _____

You say I'm

just an-oth-er bad guy; ___ you say I've

LIPS ON YOU

Words and Music by ADAM LEVINE,
JACOB KASHER HINDLIN, CHARLIE PUTH,
JULIA MICHAELS and JASON EVIGAN

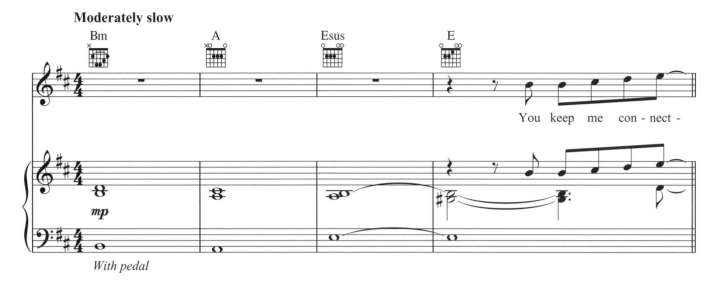

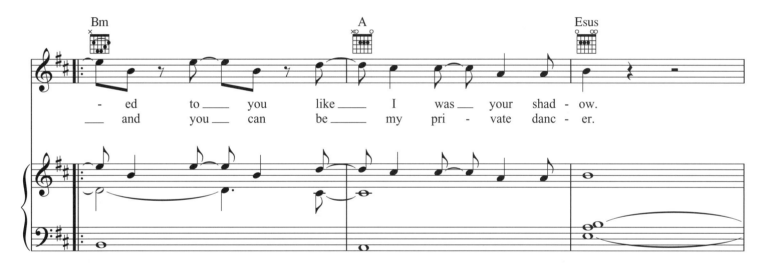

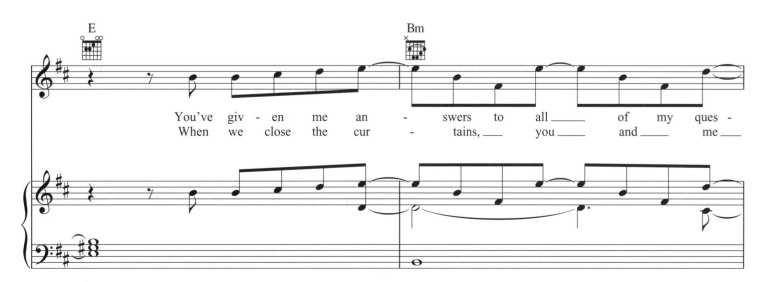

Instrumental solo

D.S. al Coda
(Take 2nd ending)

Solo ends When I put my lips on __

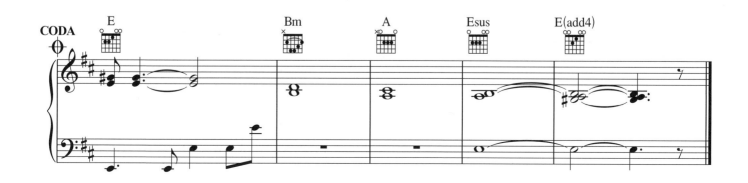

BET MY HEART

Words and Music by ADAM LEVINE,
JACOB KASHER HINDLIN, PHIL SHAOUY
and JOHN RYAN

HELP ME OUT

Words and Music by ADAM LEVINE,
THOMAS PENTZ, HENRY AGINCOURT ALLEN,
JULIA MICHAELS and JUSTIN TRANTER

*Recorded a half step higher.

WHO I AM

Words and Music by ADAM LEVINE,
TEDDY GEIGER, ERIC FREDERIC,
JACOB KASHER HINDLIN, GAMAL LEWIS,
AMMAR MALIK and JOHN RYAN

Additional Lyrics

Spoken: See, this one goes out to all the lovers,
Lovers' lovers that is,
Who spend their nights and days under covers.
Girl, the sun could burn out, but you'll still shine.
Aw, yeah.

Rap: Kiss ya, kiss ya, kiss ya, hug ya, hug ya, hug ya.
Look into your eyes, and I see the ocean.
I ain't got no wings, but you got me floatin'
On a cloud, looking down, it's emotion.
Champagne flutes, everybody toastin'.
Heart beatin' fast on this roller coaster.
Love you up and down, spin you 'round and 'round.
Can you hear me now?

WHISKEY

Words and Music by ADAM LEVINE,
JACOB KASHER HINDLIN, JOHN RYAN
and TINASHE SIBANDA

GIRLS LIKE YOU

Words and Music by ADAM LEVINE,
BRITTANY HAZZARD, JASON EVIGAN
and HENRY WALTER

Moderately fast half-time beat

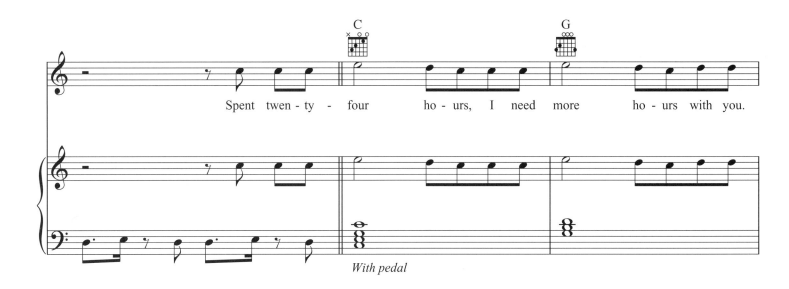

Spent twen-ty - four ho-urs, I need more ho-urs with you.

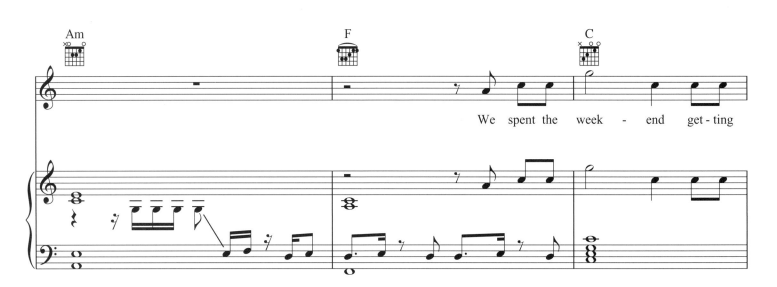

We spent the week - end get-ting

CLOSURE

Words and Music by ADAM LEVINE,
JOHN RYAN, JACOB KASHER HINDLIN,
PHIL SHAOUY and AMMAR MALIK

DENIM JACKET

Words and Music by ADAM LEVINE,
OSCAR GORRES, JAMES ALAN,
JACOB KASHER HINDLIN, TOM BARNES,
PETE KELLEHER and BEN KOHN

* Recorded a half step higher.

VISIONS

Words and Music by ADAM LEVINE,
RYAN OGREN, NICK BAILEY,
JARED WATSON and DUSTIN BUSHNELL

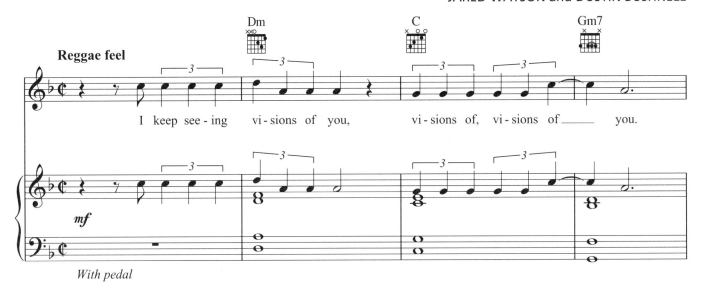

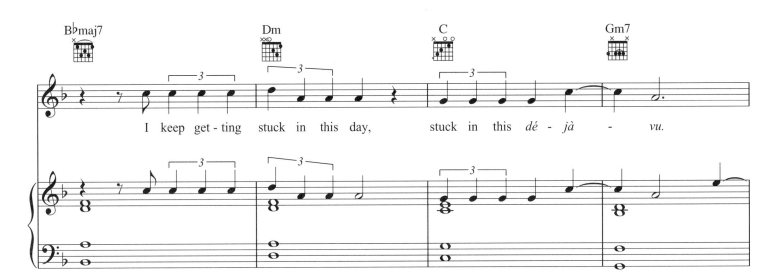

PLASTIC ROSE

Words and Music by ADAM LEVINE,
JAMES ALAN, JACOB KASHER HINDLIN
and OSCAR GORRES

DON'T WANNA KNOW

Words and Music by ADAM LEVINE,
BENJAMIN LEVIN, JOHN RYAN,
AMMAR MALIK, JACOB KASHER HINDLIN,
ALEX BEN-ABDALLAH, KENDRICK LAMAR,
KURTIS McKENZIE and JON MILLS

Additional Lyrics

Rap: No more "please stop."
No more hashtag boo'd up screenshots.
No more tryna make me jealous on your birthday.
You know just how I make you better on your birthday, oh.
Do he do you like this? Do he woo you like this?
Do he lay it down for you, touch your poona like this?
Matter fact, never mind, we gon' let the past be.
Maybe his right now, but your body's still with me, whoa.

COLD

Words and Music by ADAM LEVINE,
JOHN RYAN, JACOB KASHER HINDLIN,
PHIL SHAOUY, NOEL FISHER
and JUSTIN TRANTER

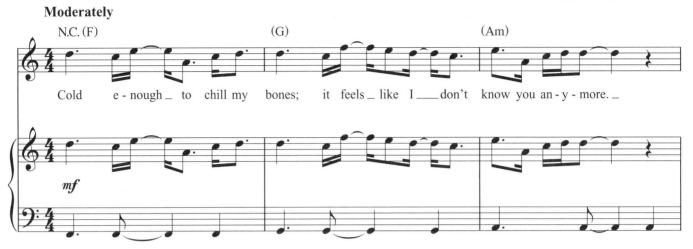

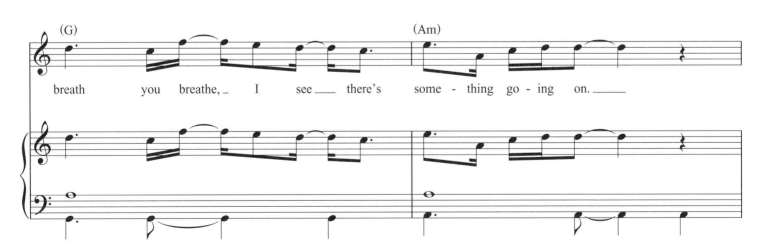